THE
Siege of Newcastle,
BY
WILLIAM LITHGOW.

Newcastle:
PRINTED BY S. HODGSON, UNION-STREET, FOR
EMERSON CHARNLEY.

MDCCCXX.

AN
EXPERIMENTALL AND EXACT
RELATION
UPON THAT FAMOUS AND RENOWNED

Siege of Newcastle,

THE
DIVERSE CONFLICTS AND OCCURRANCES
FELL OUT THERE DURING THE TIME OF TEN
WEEKS AND ODDE DAYES:

AND OF THAT

Mightie and marveilous Storming thereof,

WITH POWER, POLICIE, AND PRUDENT PLOTS OF
WARRE.

TOGETHER WITH A

SUCCINCT COMMENTARIE

UPON

THE BATTELL OF BOWDEN HILL, AND THAT VIC-
TORIOUS BATTELL OF YORK OR
MARSTON MOORE,

NEVER TO BEE FORGOTTEN.

BY
HIM WHO WAS AN EYE WITNESSE TO THE SIEGE OF NEWCASTLE,
WILLIAM LITHGOW.

Edinburgh,
PRINTED BY ROBERT BRYSON. 1645.
Cum Privilegio.

The Naval & Military Press Ltd

in association with

The National Army Museum, London

Published jointly by

The Naval & Military Press Ltd
Unit 10 Ridgewood Industrial Park,
Uckfield, East Sussex,
TN22 5QE England

Tel: +44 (0) 1825 749494
Fax: +44 (0) 1825 765701

www.naval-military-press.com
www.military-genealogy.com
www.militarymaproom.com

and

The National Army Museum, London
www.national-army-museum.ac.uk

In reprinting in facsimile from the original, any imperfections are inevitably reproduced and the quality may fall short of modern type and cartographic standards.

Preface.

THE present publication, reprinted from an original copy obligingly communicated to the editor by Sir Walter Scott, and by that eminent scholar considered to be *unique*, contains, besides the particulars of the Siege of Newcastle, some very curious and interesting details relative to the invasion of England, by the Scottish Army, in the winter of the year 1644.

The author, William Lithgow, was born at Lanerk, in Scotland, the latter end of the fifteenth century. He was originally bred a tailor; but, largely imbibing the wandering spirit of his countrymen, he felt the most insatiable desire to view distant and unknown parts of the world, and actually travelled *on foot* through Europe, Asia, and Africa. At Malaga he was thrown into the Inquisition; and the imprisonment and torture, which he there endured, entitled him in some degree to the rank of a martyr and hero.* Of his peregrinations and sufferings, he published a singularly remarkable account in the year 1614, couched in the most inflated language, and a good deal resembling in the eccentricity of its style and manner the well known "*crudities hastily gobbled up*" of the wonderful Tom Coryate.† An enlarged edition of Lithgow's work was printed in the reign of Charles the First, dedicated to that ill fated Monarch. Copies of both these editions are extremely rare.

* The crime for which he was condemned was that of being a *spy and heretic.—See Granger's Biographical History of England.*

† The reader will find a full account of this strange character in the Biographia Britannica; Wood's Athenæ Oxonienses, vol. ii. p. 208, Edit. Bliss; and Fuller's Worthies (in Somersetshire,) vol. ii. p. 290, Nichols's Edition. See also Terry's "Voyage to East India," p. 58, &c. Coryate's Book, for a century past, has been an object of competition among collectors.

Though it must be admitted the traveller, in some parts of these adventures, is apt to deal in the marvellous; yet still the particulars of the horrid cruelties, to which he informs us he was subject, have in them an air of truth. On his return from Malaga to England, he petitioned the king for redress against the Spaniards. He was in consequence soon after carried to Theobald's on a feather bed, in order that King James might be an eye witness of what he called his " martyred ana- " tomy"; meaning his wretched body mangled and reduced to a skeleton. It is said the whole court crowded to see him. The king ordered him to be taken care of; and he was twice sent to Bath at his Majesty's expense. By the royal command he applied to Gondamor, the Spanish Ambassador, for the recovery of the money and other valuable effects, of which the Governor of Malaga had plundered him; and also for a thousand pounds for his support; but, altho' he was then promised a full reparation for all the damages he had sustained, the engagement was never performed. When it was understood shortly afterwards, that that minister might probably in a little time have to leave England, Lithgow upbraided him with the breach of his word, in the presence chamber, before several gentlemen of the court. On this occasion, forgetful of the pledge that had previously been given, the perfidious Gondamor charged our traveller with having invented the whole legend. Enraged at this base subterfuge, the high minded Scot struck the ambassador; or, as he has himself expressed it, in his own odd phraseology, " contrabanded his fistuld with his fist." For this bold behaviour, the unfortunate Lithgow, although his noble spirit was generally commended, was sent to the Marshalsea, where he remained a prisoner until the ambassador's departure; a period of nine months.

At the end of the last edition of his travels, the author informs us, that in his three voyages " his " painful feet have traced over, besides passages of " seas and rivers, thirty six thousand and odd miles, "which draweth near to twice the circumference of "the whole earth." The marvellous appears here to rise to the incredible, and to place him in point of veracity below his brother tourist Coryate, to whom he has often been compared; but it is nevertheless certain that he far outwalked that celebrated Pedestrian.

Besides his travels, Lithgow published a description of Ireland, which is whimsical and entertaining. This, together with the narrative of his sufferings, is reprinted in Morgan's "Phœnix Britannicus." He also published "The present Surveigh of Lon- "don and England's State," a 4to. tract, reprinted in the 4th volume of Lord Somers's collection. He was likewise the author of "A true and experi- "mentall Discourse upon the Beginning, Proceed- "ing, and victorious Event of the last Siege of "Breda; with the Antiquity and Annexing of it to "the House of Nassau, and the many Alterations it "hath suffered by Armes and Armies, within these "three score Years;" printed in 1637, 4to.

In this interesting little volume the author alludes to his former labours, and speaks with becoming gravity of his "feet footing pedestrially," over different regions of the globe, by "several turnes "and returnes." He concludes the book with a delineation of the state of his own country, at that time overrun with the most violent zeal and party spirit. On a national question like this, on which so much may be said on either side, it is unnecessary for the Editor, on the present occasion, to express any opinion of his own. He, however, considers the description itself too characteristic to be omitted.

"Scotland, now a dayes, hath no Historian, "bravest Wits turn dull, Poets sing dumbe, Pen- "men grow deafe, and best Spirits slumber. And "why? Because there is no Mecœnas, as little re- "gard, farre less reward of ingrateful Patrones; the "praises of past worthies lie interred in the dust, "and future times robbed of the necessary know- "ledge of things past and present, and thus in the

" darknesse of ingratitude, the living men murder
" the memory of the dead. Nay, and worse, Pen-
" men now may not labour in their paines, because
" of clownish carpers, critics, calumniators, and
" distracted censurers, that tare the life of Vertue in
" pieces with their spightful tongues; for it is a
" more facile thing for a miscreant to judge than
" to suffer judgement himselfe: And especially some
" raw-mouth'd younglings, (nay rather fondlings)
" who being nearly Laureate, after short foure
" halfe yeares time spent in the colledge, they come
" forth from this small commencement, (wanting
" Wit, Judgement, and Understanding) like to
" bulls broken out from Dungeons, to beate the
" faces of the World: Wise men are ignorant to
" them, the Laiety but lubbards, old men but
" fooles; and they will have men of honour to
" honour them with the first good-morrow, the top
" of the Table, the right hand, and the enterey of
" the doore. And why? Because they are over-
" master'd with Art, not masters of it, having their

"shallow brains loaden with the empty apprehen-
"sion of bottomless syllogismes, rotten ragges of
"Heathenish Philosophy, and clouted Phrases of
"Paganisme authors, who but they? and if they
"rayle upon divine authority, vulgars say, they are
"brave Schollers, hopefull youths, and well set;
"away, runne here and there, goe beyond sea, to
"teach and concionate! Some of which presump-
"tuous crew I found here in the Leaguer before
"Breda, (I meane of mine owne countrymen, and
"none other) whose beardlesse mouths have greater
"neede of more learning, knowledge, and instruc-
"tion, than to dare to doe the thing they cannot
"doe; whose names I reserve to discover in my
"verbal and ordinary discourses."

In addition to the works before alluded to, Lithgow published a poem (Edinburgh, 1640, 4to.), entitled, "The Gushing Tears of Godly Sorrow,
"containing the Causes, Conditions, and Remedies
"of Sinne, depending mainly upon Contrition and
"Confession." This poetical effusion is dedicated

to the unfortunate James, Earl (afterwards Marquis) of Montrose; a nobleman whose admirable heroism and loyalty threw the highest blaze of splendour on his other endowments.

A portrait of the enterprizing man, of whose life and writings we have just been speaking, is prefixed to the first edition of his travels. It is a whole length, cut in Wood; representing him (with a staff in his hand) in a Turkish dress, being the garb in which he walked through Turkey. When or where poor Lithgow died the Editor has not been able to discover.

J. T. B.

Albion Place, *3d March*, 1820.

A
JUST AND EXACT DISCOURSE
UPON
The Siege and Storming
OF
NEWCASTLE,
WITH A
SUCCINCT COMMENTARIE UPON THE TWO
BATTELLS OF BOWDON HILL AND
MARSTON MOORE.

In these turbulent times, when opinions grow variable, and the diversity of doubtfull reports more voluble than the rushing winde; yet have I adventured (like to an old practicioner, in Prose, Poesie, and unparalelled peregrination,) to cast in my Myte of known Experience, upon the Brazen faces of ignorant understanders, that with the knowledge of my quotidian inspection, I may either enlighten their blindnesse, or give truth the glory of a just deserving.

And why? because now too many calumnious Criticks, being more prone to censure other mens labours, then to do any thing themselves worthie of censure, yet dare to upbraid that which hardly their sinistruous judgement can rightly construct. The world being turned to such a crabbed and crooked condition, that either they will approve what they conceive, though never so erronious, or otherwise disprove that which they affect not, though never so illustrious. Wherefore damnifying the one, and villifying the other I come to court my present purpose, and thus I begin.

> This long cross'd labour, now it comes to light,
> And I, and my discourse set in my right,
> Which reason crav'd; for where can truth prevaile,
> But where sound judgement may it countervaile.
> For what seek I? in what these times afford,
> But of my Countries praise, a just record,
> Which God allows; and what can contraires bring,
> But man for men, the light of truth may sing,
> Else after ages would be borne as blinde,
> As though our time, had come their time behinde:
> For curious Penman, and the Paper Scroule,
> They are of memorie, the life and soule.

After our first Army (levyed in the hollow time of Winter, 1644 and led by the Earl of Leven Lord

General) had with certain oppositions recoursed over Tyne, and thence falling downe to Sunderland, situate upon the River Weir (Durhams dallying and circulating consort) after, I say, they had beene provoked by the Lord Newcastle, and Lieutenant Generall King, upon the Sabboth day, to give them Battell; it was skirmished and fought two dayes together at Bowdon Hill, March 20, 21, 1644, where by the great mercy of the divine Providence, that laudable Victory fell to our Armie, and the enemie in a retyring way flying for Durham, fled shortly thereafter in a confused march unto York. To which place (their refuge) his Excellence with our Army mainly advancing, beleagured the greater halfe of the Towne; the Earle Manchester, and Lord Fairfax envyroning the rest.

Where diverse weeks and dayes being spent, in advancing their Works, their atchievements, and other approaches, there fell out (interim) certaine accidentall Skirmishes and countermatching assaults. In one of which, that mirrour of Mars and manhood, Lieutenant Colonell Ballantine was deadly wounded, whereof he dyed: A large subject have I here to handle, if time might suffer me, but true it is, hee was a Cavalier of such extraordinary fortune (being onely 28 years of age at his last vale) that in Germany, Ireland, and twice in England, hee became exceeding auspicuous in Martiall affaires, though indeed he was best understood under the name of Major Ballantine. All which discourse, and this epitomizd memoriall, I purposely abandon till a fitter time; and so I returne to my former Commentary, and thus:

This Siege of Yorke continuing still with many fortunate and misfortunate adventures, at last our severall Armies were enforced to incorporate themselves in one maine body, and that on Long-Marston Moore. Where the day following Prince Rupert imbracing their left field; our Armie upon advertisement thereof, were engaged to make a speedy returne, for rancountring the enemie, and to recover that ground which formerly they had freely forsaken: Which in the end, amongst many difficulties and mighty oppositions, they both adventerously and advantagiously obtained, to the enemies absolute overthrow, and their own victorious safety. The summarie whereof, I now involue in these following lynes, as unwilling to imbarke my selfe within the lists of intricated passages, or too peremptory and punctuall particulars; and why? because I was not there an occular Testator, and so to build upon the wings of flying report were meerly erronious, (the diversities whereof being already innumerable and incredible) but only done by way of introduction, to bring me the more facily upon the face of Newcastle, or otherwise more properly, to enlighten memorie for present and future times. And thus,

> In Iuly last, the second day and more,
> One thousand, six hundred, fourtie and foure;
> On Marston Moore, two awfull Armies met,
> Oppos'd then stood, one 'gainst another set,
> To quarrell for Religion, and that light,
> Which far excels all humane power and might,
> (And yet the darknesse of these dangrous times,
> Would faine ecclypse Gods glory, and Mens crymes,
> But here I stay, lest that in straying much,
> I gall the mighty, and the loftie touch:)
> Then cease sad Muse, returne and let me show
> This sequell stroke, for now begins the blow :
> To worke they go, well ordred on both sides,
> In stately posture; experience divides
> In Regiments and Brigads, Horse, and Foot,
> Two mightie Armies; then began to shoot,
> The roaring Cannon, and their ecchoing worce !
> Made Hills and Dales rebound their violent force,
> That fell on fatall breasts; the Musket shoures
> Went off like thunder; pryde and strife devoures
> The saiklesse standers; the naked sword and Pyke,
> Commanded crueltie, to push and strike;
> Which been obeyd, the Drum and Trumpet sounded,
> Some here some there fell downe, some deadly wounded,

On all hands there was slaughter. And what worse,
Some of our foot were troad by our owne Horse,
And Fairfax too. But true it is that course,
Brought fame to some, to others sad remorse,
Which sorrow felt; And yet our Staile stood fast,
And wrought a passage on their foes at last,
That made Opposers quake: Wings and Reserves,
By hard pursuit, on their part shortly swerves:
For Truth enraged, these Romish Butchers fled,
Gorg'd with Atheisme; their Bastard bloud they shed
Like Jezabels on ground; and there was left
For Dogs to glut on, so their lives were reft,
With admiration, that the world might see
The Heavens and Scots, gaynd both, one victorie.
Which in them was engrossd, and wondrous too,
For what could valour more for valour do
Than they that mannd this battell: It is true,
That valiant men would have a gratefull due
To cherish fame: so they our Northren hearts
(As stout as steele) dischargd their manly parts.
Where Noble Lindesay, Earl of Crawfurd now,
Stood bravely to it, made his foes to bow:
And left no ground, nor did his foote remove
Such was his courage, graft in Iesus love:
Then here his badge, which well his worth may yeeld
A Lamb at home, a Lyon in the field
And so he prov'd: where then all happie he!
Seald up his name in Tymes eternitie.
So forward Eglintoun, he actd his part,
And fiercely road, with a couragious heart
To front his foes: Where in that conflict he
Installd his name, 'mongst Peeres of Chivalrie:

Where his brave sonne, behav'd himself so well,
Some may come near, but none his worth excell:
Which if we had, as Romanes wont to have
A twofold triumph, might their merit crave.
What should I speak of Baillie, but admire.
How th' heavens his mynde, with Noble gifts inspyre,
For manners, manhood, wisedome, skill, and wit,
Both Mars and Pallas, in his bosome sit;
Their Throne, his heart, their honour, his desert
Where judgement raignes, there knowledge bears a part
And understanding too: for now these three
Crowne all his gifts, with love and modestie.
For laureat Lumsdale, fixt in Bellones camp
Procurd what hee deserves; became that lamp
Which crownes a Chiftayne: and his fame to blaze,
Still as he acts, the world may sing his praise:
There, there, he stayd, and stood so stronglie to it
Mongst mortall men, no Champion, more could do it.
Then Gallant Leslie, leader of our Trowpes
Traversd alwhere: mad spyte to valour stoupes;
Where he! adventrous he! spurrd up and downe
And cleard the field; regaynd that Delphian crowne
Which courage fought for: And what worth allowes,
A laurell Garland, may decore his browes.
Last here and there, the ground with slaughterd Corps
Was cled from York, to five adjacent Dorps:
The blood lay on the grasse like shoures of rayne
That fill the furres: the heapes of them were slaine
Like Dunghills were; that on the wearie fields
Some fought, some fled, some stood, and many yeelds:
That even me thought, the groans of Rome, and Spayne,
Were heard the coast about, on shoare and Maine:

> And father falshood, swore their Iesuit plots
> Could not prevail, gaynst our triumphant Scots:
> The enemie thus quelld, and scatterd round
> Alwhere about, nay ; some in everie ground :
> In came the Lord of Hostes, and he proclaimd
> The field was his, or what more could be nam'd
> For person, place, or time ; for he alone !
> Beat downe the Dagon, Babells Idoll Throne.
> And buryed superstition, and blynd rites :
> Within the gulf, of ever gnashing sprits :
> For which be praise, to whom all thanks and power,
> From this time forth, and so for evermore ?

Within a few dayes thereafter, upon considerable conditions, the citie of York yeelding, and the Lord Fairfax made governour thereof, our most victorious General and his redoubted army with great expedition, returned through Yorkshyre, and Bishoprick for Newcastle, to assist that Noble and judicious Chiftayne, of whom now (as it is my mayne purpose) I begin to discourse of his, and their proceedings ; and as impartially, as an honest heart may do, without either flatterie or favour.

In this last springtydes second expedition, 1644, for England ; our Parliament then sitting, Iames Earle of Calendar, Lord Almond, was selected and appoynted by them, to be Lord Lieutennant Generall of all our Scottish forces in Scotland and in England. Whereupon a considerable Armye being leuyed, consisting of six thousand foote, and eight hundred horse, he advanced for Northumberland, and courting Tweed, crossd the Tyne at Newburne. Where his Armye reposing all night, made me call to minde, these following lynes, I wrote upon that former conflict fought there foure years agoe. 1640.

> Let Conway bragge of Armes, and his great horses,
> Let Papists boast of men, and their fled coarses,
> Let Newburne rayle on Tweed, and curse their Tyne.
> Let Prelats sweare, the fault was thine and mine:
> I'le tell you newes, their Popish drifts and plots
> Were curbd and crushd, by our victorious Scots.

The day following our aforesaid armie accoasted Lumley Castle, where sojourning certaine dayes, the Lord Calendar, with a number of horse and foot (in this time) set face for Hatlepoole and Stocktoun. Where, when come, and after a promiscuous parleye, seazing upon both townes, he left garrisons there, and governours to overrule them. Whence returning to the residue of his armye, lying at Lumleye, he set forward to Osworth. From which place my Lord Calendar, sending some horse and foote to clear the way for the

Gatesyde, they were rancountred with the enemye, at the tope of the wynd mill hill, where being prevented by night, and the enemye stronger than they, they were constrained to turne back. Whereupon the next day the Lieutennant Generall himselfe, came up with the residue of his armye, and fiercelie facing the enemy, beat them from the hill, chased them downe the Gatesyde, and hushing them along the bridge, closed them within the towne. Hereupon he forthwith commanded the Gatesyde, and then the next day he begunne to dispute for the enjoying of the bridge, with the fierie service of Cannon and Musket, which indeed was manfully invaded, and as couragiously defended. Yet at last, in despight of the enemy he gained the better halfe of the Bridge, and with much adoe fortified the same with earthen Rampiers, and Artilerie, which still so defensively continued, untill the Towne was taken in by Storme. This being regardfully done, he caused to erect five Batteries, along the Bankhead, and just opposite to the Town, from whence the Cannon did continually extreame good service, not onely against the walls and batteries, but also against particular places, and particular persons: Besides the frequent shooting of Potpieces, and other fireworkes of great importance, which daily annoyed the Inhabitants within Towne: At the most of which firie imployments the Lord Calendar himself was ever personally directing them, to the which dexterity of charge, I was often both an eye witnesse and observer.

By this time, or there about, his Excellence arryving here from York, and accoasting the Tyne, he caused immediately build a Bridge over the River of Keill boats, over the which his Armie having safely and peaceably past, he caused lay downe their severall quarters with great promptitude and expedition: And so beleaguring the West and Northwest parts of the Town, they inclosed all that circuit, till they joyned with the Lord Sinclairs Regiment; Sheeffield Fort (belonging to the Town) only dividing them: And so this rebellious Town was mainly blocked up on all quarters. Now, and at this time also, the Earle Calendar recrossing Tyne, tooke presently in Sandgate, the one end whereof standing contiguat with the Towne wals. Where setting sundrie Regiments there, and about that place, he forthwith caused to construct a strong Bridge of Keill boats over Tyne (and within his quarters) for the passing and repassing of his forces to both sides, and fixed the same a pretty way below the Glasse-house. This advantagious passage became very steedable, not onely for the Souldiers, but also for the Countrey people, that brought in daily provision for the Armie. The Bridge it self (being daily guarded with my Lord Kenmoores Regiment at both ends, and a strong Centrie set at each of them within two Redoubts) had also three watrie guards of Keill boats, tyed with cable ropes, from banke to banke, to secure it from any sudden surprise.

Now as for the manner of the common Souldiers lying here in their severall Leagures, and in all parts about the Towne, their Mansions or Domiciles, I meane their Houts are composed, of Turff, Clay, Straw, and Watles. Where their Halls, Chambers, Kitchines and Cellars are all one: And yet the better sort (I mean their Officers) are overshadowed with circulating Pavillions, more ready to receive the blustring winde than the sinking raine. Then at last, all things being orderly done, and their batteries at sundrie advantages erected; then (I say) begun they to play with Cannon and Musket at others faces, and often also tempering their naked swords in others bloudy bodies: where courage cassiering despair, and valour desirous of Honour, they exposed themselves unto all hazards and dangerous attempts: Neither did they feare death (I meane our owne) more then an auspicuous fortune, for being clad with consorts, each provoked another to the uttermost of extremities; and some of them esteeming of the good Cause, more than of their owne lives, reserved the one, and lost the other. So also the inveterate enemie, making now and then diverse sallies from Towne (issuing at Posterne gates) upon our flanking trenches, engadged themselves into great jeopardies, and our Souldiers to as desperat a defence. Where indeed they both often tasted of mutuall fatalitie; till in end, the Lord Sinclairs Regiment, desygned these debording hyrelings a narrower precinct; which was, to keepe their falling bodies more safely within their sheltring walls, which indeed they constrainedly observed. For the enemy within, were more affrayed of the Lord Sinclairs Souldiers without, then of any one Regiment of the Army lying about, and they had just reason, recogitating seriously their sanguine blowes and fatall rancounters, which they disdainfully felt.

And now before I go any further, I thinke it best to shew the unacquainted Reader how the Towne is situate, from whence such mortalitie proceeded; and thus, it standeth mainly upon the devalling face of a continuing hill, falling downe

steep to the bordering River, where one narrow
street runneth along from Sandgate to Clossegate.
The Sandhill (from which the Bridge bendeth over
to Gateside) being the pryme market place, whence
the two ascending passages, court distinctly High
street, and Pilgrime street, the two chiefest streets
of the Towne; to the bowels of which, there bee
other three market places annexed. Now besides
these there are other two back streets, with five or
six *Contrades* and a number of narrow devalling
lanes. The walles about the Town are both high
and strong, built both within and without with *saxo
quadrato;* and maynely fenced with dungeon
Towres, interlarded also with Turrets, and alongst
with them a large and defensive battlement, having
eight sundry ports, and four parochiall Churches:
The which walles, the defendants within, had mar-
veilously fortifyed, rampiering them about, at most
eminent parts, with interlynings and mountaynes of
earth. The streets that were answerable to their
barrocaded Ports, and in frequent passages, were
also casten up with defensive breastworks, and
planted with Demi-culverines of irone: And above
all other workes, the towne Castle itself, was seriously enlarged, with diverse curious fortifications,
besides breastworks, Redoubts, and terrenniat

Demilunes; and withall three distinctive Horneworkes, two of which exteriourly are strongly pallosaded, and of great bounds. Nay, the very Capstone of the battlements round about the Towne, were surged and underpropd with little stones; that in case of scalleting, they might have tumbled them over upon the Assailants: Which indeed for the facility of the action, Schoole boyes might have performed. Yea, and all the gapes of the battlements, were shut up with lime and stone, having a narrow slit in each of them, through which they might murther our Souldiers, and secure themselves from a just revenge. The graffe about and without, was digged deeper, and the exteriour root of the walls, were steeply lyned with clay-mixt earth, to intercept any footing for Leddars, or climbing thereon: All the Ports about were closed with lyme and stone, and strongly barrocaded within, having no passage save at little posterne doores, where they had their quotidian intercourses.

The Townes maine constructure rysing upwards, divides it selfe in two corners, the one North at Weavers Tower, the other Southwest at Hatmakers Tower, decyphering two Hornes, like unto Calabrian Females with their bogling busks; but indeed more like unto the Novacastrians themselves, that retrogradingly adorne their Cuckolds frontespices, with the large dimension of Acteons monsterous-made hornes. Vpon the Townes Northeast side, and a little without, there was a fortresse erected, called Sheiffield Fort, standing on a moderate height, and Champion-like commanding the fields; the modell thus: It standeth squarely quadrangled, with a foure cornerd Bastion at every angle, and all of them thus quadrat, they are composed of earth and watles; having the Northeast side of one bulwarke pallosaded, the rest not, save along the top of the worke about, they had laid Masts of Ships to beat down the assailants with their tumbling force. At the entrie whereof there is a wooden drawbridge, and within it two Courts du guard, the graffe without is dry and of small importance, save onely that repugnancie of the Defendants within, which commonly consisted of three hundred men.

And now to close this Topographicall description, the invention, policie, nor wit of man, could have done more, than they did within and without for their own safetye, either for military discipline, or manly prouesses, in their owne desperat defence. Of whom our owne Countrey-men, were the cheeffest actors, both for the one and for the other; and the onely cause of so much bloodshed, and losse of lives as wee sustayned; which makes me recall this Italian proverb; *Iddio mi guarda dall' odio di mei amigi, percioche so bene a guardar mi stesto dall' odio di mei inimigi.* The Lord Keep me from the hurt of my Friends, for I know well how to keep mee from myne enemyes: A thing now adayes so frequent, that where all should stand for *amoris patriæ*, there many stand now for *doloris patriæ;* and declyning from that aunciënt and native duety *Pugno pro patria*, they involue themselves (without either honestie or honour) to extermine the lyves and libertye of their *Patria;* where strugling with their own strife, they often deservingly fall in the extreame madnesse of desperation, where now leaving them to their left selves, I revert to my purpose. The walles here of Newcastle, are a great deale stronger than these of Yorke, and not unlyke to the walles of Avineon, but especialy of Ierusalem. Being all three decored about the battlements, with litle quadrangled Turrets; the advantage resting onely upon Newcastle, in regard of seventeen dungeon Towres, fixt about the walles (and they also wonderfull strong) which the other two have not. Yet what availeth either Towres, walles, or Turrets, where the force of Armyes command; Nay, just nothing: for indeed these walles with their pendicles, were first erected to resist the Scottish invasions, and yet in vayne, for now we have shaken their foundations, and by the same strength they relyed upon, we have by the selfe same meane overthrowne them, all glorie be to the God of glorie therefore.

As for the Inhabitants resyding within, the richest or better sort of them as seven or eight Common Knights, Aldermen, Coale Merchants, Pudlers, and the like creatures are altogether Malignants, most of them being Papists, and the greater part of all I say, irreligious Atheists. The vulgar condition being a Masse of silly Ignorants, live rather like to the Berdoans in Lybia (wanting knowledge, conscience, and honesty) than like to wel disposed Christians, Plyable to Religion, civill order, or Church discipline, And why? because their bruttish desires being onely for libertinous ends; Auarice, and Voluptuousnesse; they have a greater sensualitye, in a pretended formalitye, than the savage Sabuncks with whom I leave them here engrossed: And now forsaking this present introduction, I come backe to my continewing discourse. The siege growing dayly more and more hotter and hotter, at all quarters, and in all places, as wele in the one side, as in the other; then, and at which tyme (I must ingenuously confesse) that these indefatigable pains my Lord Calendar took, were more than praise worthy, for late and early, and at all times, he was extraordinary carefull, paynefull, and diligent, in overseeing here and there his Mynes, in directing his batteryes, in managing privat and prudent ends for a publick good, in dispatching of messingers and messages, and in ordering of his souldiers atchievements, by night or by day as they were imployed; insomuch that his industrious, and vigilant actions, became a merveilous amazement; to all these that were acquainted with his paynes, and for my part, to shunne ingratitude, worthy of deserved memorie.

The chief Cannoneirs, that were upon his five batteryes in the Gatesyde, were William Hunter Captain of the trayne of Artillerie, Iames Scot, Robert Spense, and William Wallace, men of singular skill, and many more, which I purposely (to avoyd prolixitie) omit: And now from here and hence, the Lievtennant Generall traversing hourely the river to his other batteryes, and workes at Sandgate being onely two, he was ever in a fastidious action; One of which batteries, beat downe the top, face, and upmost parts of Carpenters Tower unto the dust. The other batterie had been newly erected for repulsing the enemy from intercepting our Mines. Yet notwithstanding whereof the *Nullifidians* within, discovered the lowest Myne next to the river syde: The which my Lord Calendar perceaving, and thrusting a pyke with his own hand, through the renting division, and to prevent the drowning thereof, gave presently order that the next morning it should be sprung: Which accordingly done, it tumbled over the demi-horne-wark, dissapointed the enemye, and became a shelterage to our encroaching souldiers. The other three adjacent Mynes, were not as yet reddy, neither now to be imployed as after you shall heare.

About this some time, September 29, the Lord Lieutennant generall Baillie upon the Townes north syde, and near to St. Andrews Church, gave order (for their his batterie lay) to brash downe a part of the Towne wall, which in three hours space was fortunately accomplished; where the wall fell down, within half a yard of the roote, and so large that ten men might have marched through it in a front. This tryall gave indeed a great encouragement to our Armye; and why? because then our Commanders, were assured, that if their Mynes should be dissapointed, the brashing of the walls should be their last advantage. And yet this breach was never pursued, in regard the enemie under the

shaddow of a blynd of Canvesse, reenforced, or
barrocaded it with trash and timber. Vpon Weddinsday following at morne, Octo. 3. the enemy
discovered and drowned two of our Mynes with
watter, and the next day ensuing another also.
Whereat the enemie growing insolent, gave order
for ringing of bells all night, to consolate (as it
were) the distressed mindes of the starving communaltie, who rather fed upon violent necessitie, than
any other kinde of cherishing or comfortable reliefe:
Being whiles flattered with impossibilities, and
otherwhiles tyrannized over, by the malicious malignitie of the mercilesse, and now miserable Maior.

For true it is, that this Sir Iohn Marley their
Governour, an œconomick Polititian, more wilfull
than skillfull, did so inveigle, and blindfold the
common multitude, that these letters which hee
sent to our Lord Generall, were all read by him
in publike to them, being too peremptorie and impertinent: but for the answer of his Excellence that
came to him, he concealed them all, making them
to believe, that he would admit of no condition, nor
grant any safety longer than the revenging sword,
might overreach their necks.

All which being falsly and perfidiously spoken,
was onely to irritate their doubtfull dispositions,

and to incense their desperate condition, with the deceit of a treacherous despaire, to make them bolder for their dreadfull defence: for indeed there was an order condescended upon, by the Committee, some five weeks before their ruine approached, which was, that if they should render in time, and prevent the greater effusion of bloud, they should have faire and free quarters, and all these liberall conditions, that people in the like case, could either look for, or require. But all these profers or offers, were by the Maior vilified, and by him concealed from the people, till their day of desolation was declared. And now the coppies of these intercoursing letters being lately published to the vulgar world, and striving to relinquish unnecessary particulars, or any obvious rancounter of small consequence, I come to the maine point; and thus,

After ten weeks siege and odde dayes, with many disastruous affronts, following on all hands, there was a parley appointed being Fryday October 18, where in the forenoone our three Commissioners, the Lord Humbie, the Laird of Wedderburne, and Iohn Rutherfurd Provest of Iedburgh, went in (the three Hostages from the Towne being formerly come forth) ours, I say, accoasting the Maiors presence, there were diverse propositions and answers by both parties delivered, but to no purpose nor effect. The Maior ever dallying with drifts and delayes to procrastinate time, till they had discovered our two chiefe Mines, which indeed were very near the point: yet neverthelesse (in a jeering way) our Commissioners being dismissed after five houres conference, and their Pledges returned; the next morning early the untimely preventing Maior, sent forth a Drummer, to the Lord Sinclair, with two Letters; the contents of one was thus; *My Lord, I have received diverse Letters and warrants subscribed by the name of Leven, but of late can heare of none that have seen such a man; besides, there is a strong report hee is dead: Therefore to remove all scruples, I desire our Drummer, may deliver one Letter to himselfe; Thus wishing you could thinke on some other course to compose the differences of these sad distracted Kingdomes, than by battering Newcastle, and annoying us who never wronged any of you, for if you seriously consider, you will finde that these courses will agravate, and not moderate distempers: But I will refer all to your own consciences, and rest, Your friend. John Marlay. Newcastle* 19, *October.*

Now let the judicious Reader observe, how detestable a thing it was to see this improvident man brought to such extremity, (that he could neither pitie himselfe nor yet a populous Towne) when he was just upon the point of life or death to wryte thus: for indeed long before night (for all his base derision) he knew his Excellence to be alive, and found deservyngly the smart of it: And now not to forget any maine circumstance, the Maior, the former night, recalled the Souldiers from Sheeffield Fort, to strengthen the Defendants within Towne; but ere they left the fortresse, they despightfully burned their two Courts *du guard* to the ground, and so retired: Now the sequell day come, being Saturday, October 19, (and that day which from age to age Newcastle should never forget) there were certaine commanded men, from every Regiment drawne up; The Officers, I say, having first in their owne quarters throwne the dyce, who should goe in the adventure (fewest blacks destinated thereto) they marched away to all their severall stands about the walls, againe ten of the clocke in the forenoone. Meanewhile the night before was the Earle of Calendars Cannon carried about, to supply and strengthen the four batteries that were to brash the wals, where with the rest they did exceeding good service.

Now the Mynes being ready to spring, and the

batteries brought to their greatest perfection, about three a clock in the afternoone, the two most available Mynes were sprung, one at the Whytefriers Tower Westward, and the other, neare Carres Fort, or Sandgate Eastward; (notwithstanding there were other two sprung here, one of which miscarried) so also, I say, the breaches of the walles by the batteries being made open and passable, and leddars set to at diverse parts for scalleting: Then entered mainely and manfully all the Regiments of our commanded men at all quarters, but more facily and lesse dangerous where the Mynes sprung: The greatest difficultie, and mightiest opposition, nay, and the sorest slaughter we received, was at the climbing up of these steep and stay breaches, where truely, and too truely, the enemie did more harme with hand garnads, then either with Musket, Pyke, or Herculean clubs: This Club hath a long iron-banded staffe, with a round falling head (like to a Pomegranate) and that is set with sharpe iron pikes, to slay or strike with; the forehead whereof being set with a long poynted pyke of iron; it grimely looketh like to the pale face of murther. The first of the foure breaches, was neare to Weavers Tower, where Lieutenant Colonell Henderson a Reformeir, and Major

Mophet were killed, with many others of speciall and common note. The second batterie was conjoyned with black Bessies Tower, where Major Hepburne, Captaine Corbet, Captaine Iohn Home an Edinburgensen, and that renowned Officer Lieutenant Colonell Home were slaine. The memorie of whom last now mentioned, I here in this Epitaph involue:

> Woe to that breach, beside blacke Bessies Towre,
> Woe to it selfe that bloudy butchering Bowre!
> Where valiant Home, that sterne Bellonaes blade,
> And brave Commander fell: for there he stayd
> Arraign'd by death: Where now that heart of Mars
> Deserves a Tombe, on it, a sable Herse:
> Yet here's the end of valour, (fortunes thrall)
> The most adventrous, nearest to his fall:
> And so was he: though well might he have done,
> For worth and valour, worne the Laurell crowne:
>   But this crownes all, he dyed for Christ, and more,
>   Christ now shall crowne him; with a crowne of glore.

The third batterie was contiguat with that dungeon of Westgate; where these two Captaines Iohn, and Thomas Hammiltons were slaine, with sundrie other of our Cliddisdale Regiment. The fourth and last was low by Clossegate, where the Earle Buckcleughs and Lowdons Regiments entred, both at their batteries and with scalleting leddars; whereupon their fell a fierce conflict and the falling enemye repulsed, both with the courage and resolution of our souldiers: And yet we receaved there but small losse either of Officers or others, albeit one had been too many, the divyne pleasure and providence excepted.

Now our men being enterd, and fighting for enterye at all quarters round about, Let me pause a while and consider! How grievous? And how dreadfull hot, that cruell conflict was for a long houres space: That truelie it was more than admirable! to behold the desperat courage both of the Assailants and Defendants: The thundering Cannon roaring from our batteries without, and theirs rebounding from the Castle within; the thousands of Musket balls flyeing at others faces, Like to the droving haylestones from septentrion blasts; the clangour and carving Of naked and unsheathed swords, the pushing of brangling Pykes, crying for blood; and the pittyfull clamour, of heart-fainting woemen, imploring for mercie to their husbands, themselves, and their children. That me thought (when now seriously pondered) their reverberating ecchoes piercing the clouds; that terrible noyse of fyrie incensed Martialists, and that loathsome inspection upon the brazen faces of desperation; had conjured (I say) the Heavens to confound and dissolve the earth; the earth to overwhelme the infernall Pit, the Carkases of men to lye like dead dogges upon the groaning streets: and man against man to become the object of homicidious and barbarous cruelty; O! loathsome sight of despayre. Neither was this all, for our people in this selfe tyme set a house on fire at Clossegate, whereon there fell a meritorious destruction. So had the whole Towne beene served (and a small revenge although it had beene so) if it had not beene speedily prevented by the relenting pittie of the Earle Calendar. So was there likewise at this present combustion, a Ballenger Boat set floting on the flood, full of flaming fire, (by Captaine Andrew Abirnethie) to have burned the keye-lockt ships lay there.

Insomuch that there was no policie left undone, for the destroyer to destroy destruction, nor for a speedy revenge, to bring the ruines of ruine to nothing: Yet now returning to observe my methodicall order; in this most dreadfull conflict, when the commanded Brigade of that renowned Commander the Lord Calendar, had breasted and overpassed, that blowne up Myne, connexed with

Carres fort (where Captaine Sinclair and other two of lesser note lost their lives) then I say, they marched celeriously along to the Sandhill, with flyeing collours and roaring Drummes: Meane while and at this instant, the Lieutennant generall Calendar entering the Towne, dispatched and directed, the Lord Levingston, and Killhead, the earle of Quensberryes brother, with their two Regiments to possesse the walls and to beat the enemie off, all along, betwixt and their passages unto the next breaches northwestward, which was accordingly done: So, and at this tyme, the aforesaid Brigade having attained to the Sandhill, where rancountering the exasperate enemie with a bloodie salutation, the rest of our westerne and northern Brigads, pursuing hotely these shrinking fugitives from the walles, to the choaking Market place: where being distressed (as it were) betweene Scylla and Charibdis, they presentlie called for quarters, and laying downe their Armes without assurance, some were taken, some were shaken, some stood still, and some fled away to hyde their bleeding bodyes in some secret shelter, yea; some sate downe by their fathers fire syde, as though they had caryed no armes.

Upon this surrender (the Major being formerly

fled to the Castle, with some others of greater and lesser note) they caused quickly pull downe the red flag on the Castle tope, and set up the whyte flag of peace, signifying subjection. This done, the earle Calendar, having formerly entered the Towne; with great expedition, gave presently order for quiescing of tumults, and managing disorders, after a considerable way, returned that same night to the Gatesyde. So, as he was the first lay downe before the Towne, so he was duely the first that entred it; and that to the great comfort of the Inhabitants, because of that unspeakable favour, and undeserved mercy, they then suddenly received, far beyond their merit and our expectation.

Then begun the whole Armie, commanded, and uncommanded (observing King Davids ancient rule, that they who stayd with the Baggage, and they that fought in the field, should share the booties alike) to plunder, I say, for twenty foure houres time, being an act of permission although to no great purpose. And why? because the common souldiers being onely able to plunder the common people (although they might have justly stretched their hands further) had for the greatest part of them but small benefite, excepting only housbold stuff, as bed-cloaths, linnings, Tanned leather, calve skins, men and womens apparell, pans, pots, and plates, and such like common things. But our prime Officers, I say, and others of that nature, by infringing the common souldiers, infringd themselves, and spoyled both their fortunes: for they investing themselves in the richest Malignants and papisted houses, by way of safeguard, had but small compositions for all their protection, and compelled Centries; where otherwise they might have justly and lawfully seazed upon all their enjoyments: But this ancient Proverb holdeth good here, *That Scottishmen are aye wise behinde the hand;* and so were they: And as they abused their Victorie in storming the Towne, with too much undeserved mercy, so they as unwisely and imprudently overreached themselves in plundering the towne, with an ignorant negligence, and carelesse ommission. And as they thus defrauded themselves, with a whistle in their mouths, so they pitifully prejudged, by this their inveigled course, the common souldiers of their just due, and dear bought advantages.

For by your leave, if a souldiers industrie be not quickned and animated with bountifull rewards, hee hath lesse will to performe any part of martiall service, than a dead coarse hath power to arise out of the grave: For what can bee more precious to man, than his bloud? being the fountaine and nurse of his vitall spirits, and the ground of his bodily substance, which no free nor ingenious nature will loose for nothing. And whosoever shall argument or discourse upon sound reason, and infallible experience, may easily prove and perceive, that these Commanders have ever best prospered, which have most liberally maintained and had in singular regard militarie Arts and Souldiers. Otherwise the honourable minde would account it a great deale better to have death without life, than life without reward: Yea, and the noble Commander desiring rather to want, than to suffer true worth unrecompensed.

I could instance here many examples of ingratitude in great persons, that by their too much wretchednesse to Souldiers, have first lost themselves, and then their Kingdoms, and Principalities; but I desist, onely lamenting what I saw here, the recitation of which *(amoris patriæ)* I forbear to touch: And as the Spaniard saith well, *Nella bocca serrada non ci entra las muscas;* that is, When the mouth is shut, the flees cannot enter in the throat; so saith the Italian to this same purpose, *Assai sa, che nò sa, chi sia,* hee knoweth enough that can misknow, the thing he knoweth: And the Poetick Proverb is thus,

Dic pauca, multa vide, disce quam plurima pati,
Nam multum juvant, hæc tria sæpe viros.

Speake little, see much, learne to suffer more,
For these three oft, help men, the world all o're.

And now closing these comparisons, I proceed to my methodicall discourse. As for the number of our souldiers, that were lost at the storming of this obstinate and unhappie Towne (not reckoning the fatalitie of other times) they extended to three hundred lacking one; of whom there were thirtie eight Officers of six distinctive kindes, besides seven or eight hundred, that were diverse wayes ill hurt, of which wounds, some have lately dyed since that time. And now I recall, that these three sieges of Breda, York, and now Newcastle, were all of one dyet, though not at one time, and did each of them so nearly sympathize one with another, in the computation of ten weekes and odde dayes, that they may all three rest now contented, to live under the substant shadow of an honest and honourable subjection. Yet when I consider here the malicious obstinacie of Newcastle, and thereupon the storming of it, I am ravished with admiration to behold, how in the heat of bloud, and goaring slaughter, they got so soon mercie and quarters; that me thinketh there was not the like mercie showne in such a case, since the deluge of the World. Nay, and (alas) showne unto an impenitent and pernicious people: When contrariwise, the lives and goods of man, wife and child, within that refractarie Towne, (for their railing and blasphemie dailie abounded) were in the power and pleasure of our victorious Armie. The which favour I dare avouch, may be a paterne to all succeeding ages enduring time, for pity, pardon, and piety.

And to instance heere the contrary example, you shall see, and that within these twenty years past, how the populous and once famous City of Madenburg in Germany, (being all Protestants) was beleagured with the imperiall forces. Whereafter diverse parleyes, and subtile drifts, the enemie on a sudden stormed the Town, where forthwith they slew eleven thousands, of men, woemen, and children: and the next morning, their divelish despight, growing wearie of that murdering slaughter, unnaturally, and unmercifully, threw headlong eighteene thousands of them in the River: So that none escaped in the whole City of young or old, save onely foure hundred that fled into a Church. And striping these starke naked, sent them away, and plundering all the goods of the Towne, at last razed it to the ground.

By which crueltie this famous Universitie, as it was first sacked, and then burned with fire, so the people were both slayne with the sword, and drowned with the watter; O pittifull destruction. And that river which formerly had brought them profit and pleasure, was then suddenly become their death and sepulture.

> This fragrant flood! that wont to serve and please,
> Their trade with gayne, their paines with pleasant ease;
> Yea; filld their hearts with pleasure, beauteous strayes,
> To see a River, passing free allwayes.
> The banks along adornd, with stately trees
> That daylie payd, kynd tribute to their eyes;
> Where flourie Meeds, round hills, salubrious fields,
> Enclosed this closure, and their Custome yeelds
> With swelling brookes to help it. This rare Piece!
> Became more sweet, than Tempian streames in Greece;
> And gracd their Schooles and science, lib'rall Arts,
> Where learning floorishd, Vertue light imparts.
> Yet fatall Elue, was now thy glutting wombe,
> That fed their lust with fish, become their Tombe,
> And swallowing grave? Art thou sad dismall bounds
> That plunging sepulcher; ingulfd with wounds
> Hatchd from thyne Euripus; gaynst Natures tract
> As death had summond thee, to doe this fact.

> No, no, I grant (this losse) their detriment,
> Sprung not from thee, dumb sensles element;
> But from these cruell hands, that straind thy strength
> To murder natures glorie, Where at lenth
> They sunk within thy bosome; then! thou roard
> And all thy brinks about, their fall deplord;
> And sought the Heavens, as Iudges to revenge
> This Parracide, and that slayne Cities change.

Now miserable Newcastle! what canst thou say? that was not dealt at all with such tyranicall crueltie, when thou hadst deserved a worser destruction than they, who stood out onely for Religion, you having litle or none at all. Then what shall I say, but that your desolation may come yet on a sudden, unlesse you amend your wicked lives, and with Ninivie turne to the Lord with prayer and fasting. Ever acknowledging the great goodnesse and clemencye of Scots-men, so undeservingly exposed upon you a headstrong and sedicious people. Yet notwithstanding whereof, thy sydes are shaken and torne, thine edges broken downe, and the burden of thy miserie, lying sore upon thy shrinking shoulders. Which makes me now call to minde, the miserable effects of warre (howsoever deservinglie fallen upon thee) the nature of which, I here involve in these lynes.

O woefull warre! that lessens wealth and strength,
And brings the ruines of ruine at lenth:
It doth dishonour honour, and degrade
The mightie man from what his greatnesse had:
Then quells the poore, and spoyles the pleasant lands
Where peace and pleasure, joynd with other hands:
Which weight let Tyrus, sometimes stately plumd,
With Troy and Thebes, both alike consumd:
Swelld Ninivie, whose fragments nought imparts,
And learned Athens, once the source of Arts:
With slightlesse Carthage, Lacedemon rent,
Jebus, and Bagdat, in a manner shent;
Sardis, Syracuse, Adrianople lost!
Nay? now stressd Almaine, with such sorrows crost;
(And Britanes Ile, the Irish bounds, and Spayne
Where thousands fall, and many thousands slaine:)
Denote and shew, what tyme and warres have wrought
That crushd their might, from flattring pryde to nought:
Nay; Monarchies, great Kingdomes, th' Vniverse
Are prest to change, erectd, throwne downe by Mars:

Like to the rage of the impetuous flood,
Debording from his banks; leaves slyme and mood
To choake the fertile playnes; supplants the rootes,
Of hearbes and Trees; defaceth quyte the fruits
Of grapes and grayn; and often breaks the walls
Of strongest Townes, whereon destruction falls.

Even so the furye, of the bloodie warre
In breaking downe the bonds of peace: debarre,
The links of love and alliance: quite defaceth
The libertie of Nature; and disgraceth:
The ornaments of tyme; And cuts the throat,
Of martiall Darlings; then casts up the lot

> Of desolation ; which destroyeth all
> That can to meane, or mighty men befall:
> So, so, Newcastle, to it selfe became,
> A treachrous foe, when friends besiegd the same.

And I may not forget here, how a despightfull jest, was suddenly revolved in sad earnest, that even when, the Towne was a storming, there was a childe baptized, and a number of thirty persons at the baptisme feast; I meane in Newcastle : And making merrie with the best cheare they had, they begunne to drink a health about the Table; and that was, to the confusion of the Scots rebells, and knew of no danger, till a dosson of our souldiers came in upon them (to digest their confused health) with drawn swordes and Pistolls. At which, the rayling and jeering Tablers, falling downe beneath the boord (as it were) distracted of their wits : our adventurers fell a plundering their pockets, leaving the greatest part of them stript of their apparrell, and the house utterlie spoyled of domestick furniture, and with this salve they solmnized their frolick feast : Being (I say) a just reward, for such a malicious misregard.

Now the Towne being ours, upon Sunday morning, October. 20. 1644. his ever happy and auspicuous excellence, entered the Towne, a triumphant

Victor, and repairing to S. Nicholas Church accompanyed with the Earle of Calendar, Lieutennant-generall Baillie, and the generall of Artillerie, with a few others (for it was not a day for men of fortune to dalleye with time) there was thankes given to God (by that reverend Pastor Master Robert Dowglas) for that our famous, and renowned Victorie. And now to seale up all, the clouds fell impetuously a weeping three dayes together, for that great fatalitye (as I may say) of so many brave Cavaliers as we lost. And with this same deluge, the two Keill bridges, above, and below, were broke downe, and dissenabled for passage, with the violent rapt of Tynes debording streame: But happye it was that the greatest part of our armie got then shelterage within the Town, otherwise they had found by this dissoluing rayne sommersed quarters.

Vpon the fourth day after the towne was stormed, there issued from the Castle, three score twelve Officers, Ingeniers, and prime Souldiers, under the custodie of our Perforce; and were incarcerat within the Towne, as many of their kinde were served so before. The Maior, and some of our noble Countreymen, were also then dismissed from the Castle, but not enlarged, and the day following (being Wednesday) the Maior was returned from his house, unto a Dungeon trance within the Castle: Where now that presumptuous Governour remaineth, till the Hangman salute his neck with a blow of Straffords courtesie; where now I leave him till he enjoy his merit.

As for the number of the enemie, either souldiers or Townesmen, that carried armes during the siege, indeed it is no part of my intention to medle with them, although they medled too much with us, neither with their hungrie Troupers, and far worse their hungred Horses. Yet neverthelesse (as I was informed) they were but eight hundred of the Traind Band, and some nine hundred besides, of Voluntiers, prest-men, Coliers, Keill-men, and poore trades-men; with some few experimented Officers to overtop them, which were at last overtopped themselves.

And now meanewhile we found great penurie and scarcitie of victuals, amunition, and other necessaries within this dejected Towne; so that they could not have holden out ten dayes longer, unlesse the one halfe had devoured the other. And now the encroaching Winter, commanding expedition, our Armie was sent to their Garrisons abroad (reserving onely a proper Garrison for Newcastle) some to Darnton, Haulkland, Durham, Chester,

Morpet, Exome, and other near adjacent places. Yet neverthelesse the plague was raging in Gatesyde, Sandgate, Sunderland, and many countrey Villages about. Vpon the eight day after the taking of Newcastle, the Lord Generall rode downe to Tinmouth Castle; where after a short parley, young Sir Thomas Riddell Governour thereof, surrendred it upon easie conditions. The occasion why, was thus, the Pestilence having been five weeks amongst them with a great mortalitie, they were glad to yeeld, and to scatter themselvs abroad; but to the great undoing and infecting of the Countrye about, as it hath contagiously begun.

And now before I draw to Finis, I must water my muse a little in the Poeneian springs, and gargarizing her throat with Newcastle, I will bath her old inventions in Permessis streame, fixt under that Heliconean forked hill; where Soron breasting Parnassus, saluteth with the pleasures of Pindus, all aged Poets, as I am now in my Climaterick yeare.

> Now in this Treatise, thou hast seen the Mappe
> Of revolution, and that sudden clappe
> Of ever changing Tyme, and how the fates
> And sterne-facd destinie, ramverse the Mates
> Of stubbornnes and pryd: and how the wind,
> Brecks downe the talest Cedar, that we find

On Libans flowrie banks; and how the Oake
Though fensd with boughs, must yeeld unto the stroake
Of a septentrion blast; Heavens Constellations
Concurrd in one, to judge these execrations
Flew forth from steep-bankd Tyne; what filthie rayling,
Brust from her gutts? even when we were assailing
Her girded sides with walls: That even me thought,
Sterne Radamanthus, had their forgings wrought:
Then in came Iudgement, in this cracking thunder
And fac'd with terrour, did produce a wonder,
That vomits spyte and blood: Next headlong comes
(Backd with shrill Trumpets, and lowd roaring Drummes,)
Base stinking pryde quite stript: where being naked
The shryne of fortune blushd, and blindnesse quaked.

But now to wheele about! behold, and see,
The divyne Iustice, with an awfull eye
Declaring sentence, punishment, and yoake,
To thrall their necks, with a correcting stroake.
How long did pittie knock, at their shut gate?
And offerd mercy, to their desprat state
Yet would they not receave't; nor could they pitty
Themselves, brought under, a judiciall dittie:
But sufferd death to stand, where justice stood
And they Delinquents, to a gen'rall good:
Yet in came Mercy, from their friendly foes
And pleaded for their pardon: Mercie goes
Along with us to them; which, when they see,
They grew ashamd, to finde such clemencie.
For what sought we, but their desyred good?
And to prevent, the effusion of blood
Proposd them courteous proffers, all to wonne,
Their Hearts and Soules, to seek salvation:

And to professe that word (Religions Lamp)
Where light and Truth, have both one heavenlie stamp:
Yet this they would not, and as hardly will,
Consent, unforcd, to leave their froward ill:
Now vanquishd they, and from their dutye swervd
May sweare, our Scots, shew mercie undeservd
To hardned hearts like flint: and what rests more,
But practise must the fall of pride deplore
Which cankerd Natures keeps: But they're so blinded,
As if disdayne, had all their malice winded
With stiffnesse and contempt: yet for their words
Sometymes they're fair, and sometimes sharp like swords:
But what is that, we have them under feet,
And needs not weigh their breath, be't sowre or sweet.
For where the victors rule, the vanquisht stand,
Like Bajazet, to Tamberlanes strong hand,
And freedome thrald, by just disdaine, then pryde
Stoupes like a slave, the sword must things decyde.
Yet mercy keeps some measure, curbing reason,
With generous lenitie, actd out of season.
Yea, sometimes its more honest; for to saue,
Than to expide, the vanquisht to the grave:
What though they bark like to Hircanian Doggs,
Or bleeting stand, like winter-beaten Hogges
Yet there's compunction, and reuenge to use
(Accordingly) as tymes may time excuse:
And sealing mercie, with a sworded hand,
Makes foes, more loath to flie, than forcd to stand.

And now to close the summary of this tragicall discourse, I heartily beseech Almightie God, to

preserve and prosper our Armie; and to be their
guard, guide, and Governour, whithersoever they
go, and to imprint the feare of his holy Name in
their hearts. And now most good and gracious
Lord, blesse so and sanctifie the hearts of their chief
Commanders and Leaders, with wisedome, courage,
and magnanimity of minde; that they never decline,
neither to the right nor to the left hand; but keep-
ing a straight course, in Honour, honesty, and
holinesse; they may ever in all their proceedings,
have the glory of thy great and glorious Name
before their eyes, that the life and light of Peace
and Truth may in all true beleevers abound.
Amen.

FINIS.

www.ingramcontent.com/pod-product-compliance
Lightning Source LLC
LaVergne TN
LVHW011413080426
835511LV00005B/522